Keep this pocket-
you are visiting St.
the locality.

Whether you are in your car or on foot, you will enjoy an evocative journey back in time. Compare the Stafford of old with what you can see today— see how the streets of the town and its parks and open spaces have changed; examine the shops and buildings and notice how they have been altered or replaced; look at fine details such as lamp-posts, shop fascias and trade signs; and see the many alterations to Stafford and its surrounding villages that have taken place unnoticed during our lives, some of which we may have taken for granted.

At the turn of a page you will gain fascinating insights into Stafford's unique history.

FRANCIS FRITH'S
pocket ALBUM

STAFFORD
LIVING MEMORIES

A POCKET ALBUM

Adapted from an original book by
FIONA SHERIDAN

First published in the United Kingdom in 2005 by
Frith Book Company Ltd

ISBN 1-85937-952-4
Text and Design copyright © Frith Book Company Ltd
Photographs copyright © The Francis Frith Collection

The Frith photographs and the Frith logo are reproduced under licence from Heritage
Photographic Resources Ltd, the owners of the Frith archive and trademarks

British Library Cataloguing in Publication Data

Stafford Living Memories - A Pocket Album
Adapted from an original book by Fiona Sheridan

Frith Book Company Ltd
Frith's Barn, Teffont,
Salisbury, Wiltshire SP3 5QP
Tel: +44 (0) 1722 716 376
Email: info@francisfrith.co.uk
www.francisfrith.co.uk

Printed and bound in Great Britain by MPG, Bodmin

Front Cover: **STAFFORD, THE SWAN HOTEL** c1955 / S411056
The colour-tinting is for illustrative purposes only, and is not intended to be historically accurate.

Frontispiece: **STAFFORD, MARKET SQUARE** c1955 / S411087

AS WITH ANY HISTORICAL DATABASE THE FRITH ARCHIVE IS CONSTANTLY
BEING CORRECTED AND IMPROVED AND THE PUBLISHERS WOULD WELCOME
INFORMATION ON OMISSIONS OR INACCURACIES

MARKET SQUARE c1955 / S411022

CONTENTS

FRANCIS FRITH
VICTORIAN PIONEER

Francis Frith, founder of the world-famous photographic archive, was a complex and multi-talented man. A devout Quaker and a highly successful Victorian businessman, he was philosophic by nature and pioneering in outlook. By 1855 he had already established a wholesale grocery business in Liverpool, and sold it for the astonishing sum of £200,000, which is the equivalent today of over £15,000,000. Now in his thirties, and captivated by the new science of photography, Frith set out on a series of pioneering journeys up the Nile and to the Near East.

INTRIGUE AND EXPLORATION

He was the first photographer to venture beyond the sixth cataract of the Nile. Africa was still the mysterious 'Dark Continent', and Stanley and Livingstone's historic meeting was a decade into the future. The conditions for picture taking confound belief. He laboured for hours in his wicker dark-room in the sweltering heat of the desert, while the volatile chemicals fizzed dangerously in their trays. Back in London he exhibited his photographs and was 'rapturously cheered' by members of the Royal Society. His reputation as a photographer was made overnight.

VENTURE OF A LIFE-TIME

By the 1870s the railways had threaded their way across the country, and Bank Holidays and half-day Saturdays had been made obligatory by Act of Parliament. All of a sudden the working man and his family were able to enjoy days out, take holidays, and see a little more of the world.

With typical business acumen, Francis Frith foresaw that these new tourists would enjoy having souvenirs to commemorate their days out. For the next thirty years he travelled the country by train and by pony and trap, producing fine photographs of seaside resorts and beauty spots that were keenly bought by millions of Victorians. These prints were painstakingly pasted into family albums and pored over during the dark nights of winter, rekindling precious memories of summer excursions. Frith's studio was soon supplying retail shops all over the country, and by 1890 F Frith & Co had become the greatest specialist photographic publishing company in the world, with over 2,000 sales outlets, and pioneered the picture postcard.

FRANCIS FRITH'S LEGACY

Francis Frith had died in 1898 at his villa in Cannes, his great project still growing. The archive he created continued in business for another seventy years. By 1970 it contained over a third of a million pictures showing 7,000 British towns and villages.

Frith's legacy to us today is of immense significance and value, for the magnificent archive of evocative photographs he created provides a unique record of change in the cities, towns and villages throughout Britain over a century and more. Frith and his fellow studio photographers revisited locations many times down the years to update their views, compiling for us an enthralling and colourful pageant of British life and character.

We are fortunate that Frith was dedicated to recording the minutiae of everyday life. For it is this sheer wealth of visual data, the painstaking chronicle of changes in dress, transport, street layouts, buildings, housing, engineering and landscape that captivates us so much today, offering us a powerful link with the past and with the lives of our ancestors.

Computers have now made it possible for Frith's many thousands of images to be accessed almost instantly. The archive offers every one of us an opportunity to examine the places where we and our families have lived and worked down the years. Its images, depicting our shared past, are now bringing pleasure and enlightenment to millions around the world a century and more after his death.

STAFFORD

AN INTRODUCTION

Stafford today is a county town of about 60,000 people; it is situated in the fertile valley of the river Sow, a tributary of the River Trent, which it joins at Great Haywood. To the north lies the city of Stoke-on-Trent, famous for its pottery industry, while to the south lies the industrialised conurbation of Birmingham and the Black Country. The landscape around Stafford is mainly rural and dotted with villages large and small; nearly all of them can trace their history back many centuries. Immediately to the south lies the upland plateau of Cannock Chase, once a royal hunting forest, at times the scene of industries such as iron working, glass making and coal mining, but now covered by forest and heath, and designated as an Area of Outstanding Natural Beauty. On its eastern flank sits Rugeley, a former market and coal-mining town, dominated by the cooling towers of its power station.

Man has occupied the region since prehistoric times. Archaeological and environmental evidence points to the clearance of woodland from the sixth millennium BC. Bronze Age people buried their dead in round barrows on Tixall Heath, but the most impressive remains of our earliest ancestors are the defensive Iron Age hill-forts at Castle Ring on Cannock Chase and at Bury Ring near Stafford: these are large open hill-top enclosures surrounded by high banks and ditches. The Roman Watling Street, the present A5, passes to the south, but recent excavations in Stafford have revealed evidence of several Roman granary structures and some pottery.

Stafford lies on an island of sand and gravel surrounded by river and marsh, with the route from the north the only natural causeway. According to tradition, in the 8th century St Bertelin built a hermitage on the 'Isle of Bethney', which has been identified as Stafford. In AD 913 Aethelflaed, the daughter of King Alfred, fortified Stafford during the campaign to drive the Danish armies from the region, and within this area people settled and traded. Coins were minted here by AD 930, and a pottery industry flourished – it exported its wares to Worcester, Hereford and Chester. By AD 1000 the small wooden church had been rebuilt in stone, and the settlement had become the administrative centre of the new county.

Nearly all the places mentioned in these pages appear in the Domesday Book of 1086, a survey of land undertaken for William the Conqueror, which records that Stafford had a hundred and seventy-nine houses. The new Norman landowners built castles, such as the one near Stafford, to assert their authority and to protect their interests. Even the Bishop of Lichfield had a fortified residence at Eccleshall Castle by 1200.

The earth and timber defences around Stafford were extended and replaced by a wall with gates, through which the main routes entered the town. The line of these walls and the sites of the gates are preserved today in many of the street names. The centre of life for many centuries was the market. Here people from the surrounding countryside came on foot or with carts to buy and sell goods and livestock, meet friends and exchange news and gossip. By the mid 13th century, Stafford, Rugeley and Eccleshall had all been granted the right to hold weekly markets, as well as fairs.

Many parish churches were built or rebuilt between the 12th and 13th centuries. Some of those illustrated here, although sometimes over-restored in the 19th century, are amongst the finest in the county: St Chad's in Stafford and St Lawrence in Gnosall with their beautiful Norman carving, Holy Trinity in Eccleshall, described as the most perfect 13th-century church in the county, and the large Collegiate Church of St Mary in Stafford.

In the mid 16th century, Henry VIII dissolved the monasteries and stripped away much of the land and privileges of the church. Much of this land was sold or given to courtiers, many of whom proceeded to build large houses and to develop their estates. Sir William Paget, a privy counsellor, acquired much of Cannock Chase: here he built his mansion, Beaudesert Hall, now demolished, and developed an iron-smelting industry in the Rising Brook Valley, near Rugeley. The large quantities of wood required for the charcoal used in the furnaces resulted in much of the Chase becoming deforested by 1610.

In September 1642, just after the start of the Civil War, King Charles and Prince Rupert stayed in Stafford for two days while on their way to Shrewsbury. In March 1643, at the battle of Hopton Heath close to Stafford, the Royalists defeated the Parliamentarian army. In May, however, some Parliamentary forces crept into the town under cover of darkness, secured it, and arrested the Royalist leaders. In June the Parliamentarian army turned to Eccleshall, and besieged the Royalist Bishop in his castle. When they finally entered in August, they found a trunk of plate worth several thousand pounds, forty barrels of ale and the body of the eighty-three year old bishop, who had died the week before!

Celia Fiennes visited Stafford in 1698 and described it as 'an old built town timber and plaister pretty much in long peaked rooffes of tiling'. Up until this time most of the houses in the towns as well as the villages were timber-framed; some of them still survive, and can be seen in these photographs. There was an ever-present danger of fire, however, amongst timber buildings, and Rugeley suffered two extensive fires in 1649 and

1709. From the 18th century onwards, brick became the main building material in the area.

Roads, then later canals and railways, followed the valley of the River Trent and exerted a considerable influence on the towns and villages they passed through or by-passed. The medieval London to Chester road, the present A51, ran from Lichfield to Stone through Rugeley, Colwich and the Haywoods, while another route led through Eccleshall. With the improvement in road conditions after turnpike trusts were set up to maintain them during the 18th century, coach traffic throughout the country increased. Coaches needed to stop for fresh horses, and passengers needed food and accommodation, so inns at places along the routes, such as in Stafford and Eccleshall, became busy, prosperous places. The coming of the railway, which linked Stafford with Birmingham by 1837, resulted in the collapse of this trade. Eccleshall was by-passed by both the canals and the railway, and its failure to develop after this has helped to preserve its handsome main street.

Entrepreneurs such as Josiah Wedgwood, founder of the famous pottery firm, were enthusiastic supporters of canal building. The Trent and Mersey Canal and the Staffordshire and Worcestershire Canal, which joined at Great Haywood, were both engineered by James Brindley, and completed by 1777. By 1790 boats could travel all the way from Liverpool to London through Staffordshire, and goods of all sorts could be transported much more easily and cheaply than before.

Iron had been worked in and near Rugeley since medieval times, and coal mining had begun by 1814, although at this time the main manufacture in the town was hat making! In Stafford the shoe making industry, which was begun around 1780 by William Horton, was becoming important. His friend Richard Brinsley Sheridan, the dramatist, and MP for Stafford from 1780 until 1806, proposed the toast 'May the manufactures of Stafford be trodden underfoot by all the world'. The number of manufacturers increased, all of whom relied on outworkers in Stafford as well as Gnosall and Eccleshall; they made up shoes in their homes and returned them to the warehouses, where they collected further supplies of leather. From the 1860s, sewing machines were introduced, and most work took place in factories, mainly to the north of the town.

Stafford grew rapidly from a population of about 4000 in 1801 to 14,437 in 1871. Problems common to other industrial areas developed, such as poor sanitation, bad drainage and lack of a good water supply. A judge in 1870 declared that Stafford was 'the most stinking town I was ever in in my life'. The search for a new water supply, which was eventually found near Milford, led to the discovery of brine; this was piped into the town and used for the Brine Baths built in 1892. Efforts to improve the drainage of the river by the construction of a new weir and reclamation of land eventually resulted in the opening of Victoria Park.

Much of the countryside around Stafford belonged to major landowners, who farmed their estates and landscaped their grounds. At Shugborough, the Anson family moved the inhabitants of the original village to Great Haywood, as it spoiled their view. A later descendent allowed the construction of the railway through his land, only providing that it was hidden from his view and that trains would stop at Colwich when requested; whereas his neighbour Sir Charles Wolseley refused to let them cross his land at all!

In late 19th century, shops became more numerous along the main streets of the towns, selling a wide range of goods. Some of those we see in these photographs opened at this time, and survived until fairly recently. By 1900 local shops, particularly grocers and provision dealers, were facing competition from the early multiple stores such as Lipton's, the Co-operative stores and the Maypole Dairy, all of whom sold a basic range of good quality cheap provisions.

During the 20th century shoe making declined in importance, while engineering increased. Alstom (previously GEC and English Electric) is still a major employer in Stafford, which also remains an important administrative centre. In Rugeley coal-mining continued, and in 1960 a new pit at Lea Hall was opened; it was supposed to provide work for a hundred years, but it closed in 1990. Although agriculture characterises the surrounding landscape, villages such as Eccleshall and Hixon now have industrial estates.

The two World Wars left their mark on the area: prisoner-of-war and military training camps were created on Cannock Chase, and airfields, such as at Hixon, were laid out - most of them are now disused. After the Second World War, ambitious plans were put forward to improve towns by large-scale programmes of council house building, the construction of new roads and by-passes, and the redevelopment of town centres with better shopping and leisure facilities. As we look through these photographs, we can see how some of these aims were put into practice during the 1950s and 1960s.

The photographs show a transitional stage, when long-established local shops stood alongside chain stores such as Woolworth's, Boots, Marks and Spencer and Burton's. In both Rugeley and Stafford at that time, grocery shops stand on the main streets, whereas now there are none; they have all been replaced by supermarkets surrounded by large car parks near the edge of the town centre.

Leisure activities, too, have changed, and recreation has given a new life to other areas and buildings today. The growth of canal cruising has led to the continued upkeep and improvement of the canals. The Ancient High House in Stafford has been restored and opened as a museum, and Stafford Castle has been excavated, with trails laid out around the medieval earthworks, and a visitor centre has opened. Shugborough Hall, which now has a museum and a rare breeds farm, is a popular attraction at weekends for the enjoyment of events such as open air concerts and craft fairs.

As we look through these pages we will see much that is still familiar, while other features or places have changed or disappeared. Most of our towns and villages have long histories, and they have been continually changing or developing - although it can sometimes feel that this has happened more rapidly in the last fifty years than previously!

The elegant, classical façade of the Shire Hall has dominated the Market Square since it was built in 1798, replacing an earlier Elizabethan hall. It housed the county and assize courts and the meetings of the magistrates, and from 1972 until 1991, the Crown Court. It is now occupied by the Art Gallery and the Library. To the right are the offices of the Paramount Building Society and the Co-operative Insurance Society above the Midland Bank.

MARKET SQUARE

C1955 / S411011

The market was held in the square from at least the 12th century until 1853, when a new covered hall was built behind the Guildhall. When this was requisitioned as a food store during the Second World War, stalls once again occupied the Market Place. In 1953 it was laid out with seats and gardens to commemorate the Queen's coronation.

THE TOWN CENTRE

C1965 / S411110

In 1737 a Stafford mercer, John Stevenson, started a bank, one of the earliest outside London. As other banks opened it became known as the Old Bank, the name seen here on the building to the left of the Shire Hall. In 1866 it merged with Lloyds Bank, who still occupy the premises.

MARKET SQUARE

c1965 / S411090

MARKET SQUARE

c1960 / S411094

The flag flies over the Guildhall, which was built in 1934-5. Underneath the stained glass windows of the council chamber we can see the arcade of shops leading to the Market Hall, flanked by Marley Modes, a ladies' dress shop, and Bradleys, a gentlemen's outfitters. The extensive bus shelters and the railings of the underground public lavatories can be seen in the foreground.

MARKET SQUARE

c1960 / S411087

Here we can see the proximity of the medieval St Mary's Church to the market place. Through the centuries, the Square was the setting for many fairs, parades and celebrations. In 1800 the local newspaper reported that a chimney sweep had auctioned his wife there for 5s 6d!

Well-known stores occupy buildings of very different periods. F W Woolworth's, with its large window display and traditional sign, occupies a building which dates back to the 15th century, while the foundation stones of Burton's menswear shop, with its flamboyant sign, were laid in 1935 by Henry Montague Burton and Stanley Howard Burton.

MARKET SQUARE

c1955 / S411033

In the 16th century, when one of the town's wells stood in the Market Square, by-laws were introduced which warned that 'no persons shall wash any clothes, fish, water horses, or wash parsnips in at or near any common well'. This street scene, looking towards the ornate timber-framed building of the Ancient High House, shows buildings of different periods and styles. The most modern of these is Boots the chemist, which had recently replaced an earlier timber-framed shop. In the foreground pedestrians are crossing at traffic lights, while others queue in the bus shelters to the left.

MARKET SQUARE

c1960 / S411089

In the foreground, awnings are pulled out over Briggs shoe shop and the Maypole Dairy. Next door, under the clock, is Mottrams, established in 1865. It was a pawnbrokers, and later it sold clothes and jewellery. The clock tower of the Brine Baths stands toward the end of the street, where the road is congested with buses and lorries.

GREENGATE STREET

C1955 / S411084

The printing and bookbinding business occupies the upper floors above W H Smith's and Greenwoods, a ladies' outfitters. Further down the street we can see the distinctive sign of the Bear Inn. This stands on the site of the White Bear, which was a busy coaching inn in the early 19th century with coaches travelling to London, Birmingham and Liverpool.

GREENGATE STREET

c1955 / S411086

THE ANCIENT HIGH HOUSE

1948 / S411010

This large, timber-framed house was built around 1595 by the wealthy Dorrington family. King Charles I and Prince Rupert stayed here in 1642, but later in the Civil War it was used as a prison for Royalist officers. During the 1780s it was occupied by Dr Thomas Fowler, a physician at the Infirmary. He developed an arsenic solution to treat patients with 'agues, remitting fevers and periodic headaches'. As 'Fowlers Solution' it became a popular medicine in Victorian times, and was used to treat everything from asthma to rheumatism, as well as being used as a cosmetic face wash!

*By 1800 this had become the main coaching inn of Stafford, and coaches
left for Manchester, Bristol, Chester, Liverpool, Birmingham and London.
In 1825 George Borrow, author of 'Romany Rye', described it as 'a place of
infinite life and bustle', but when Charles Dickens stayed in 1852, several
years after the railway had destroyed the coach trade, he wrote about it as 'the
extinct town-inn, the Dodo'. By 1924 it was recommended by both the AA
and the RAC, and the stables had become garages. A policeman is directing
traffic coming out of the street on the right.*

THE SWAN HOTEL

C1955 / S411056

ST CHAD'S CHURCH

c1955 / S411009

The river Sow surrounds Stafford on three sides. This is the Green Bridge, over which traffic had to pass before entering through the Green Gate in the medieval walls. Note the small shops along the front of the Baths, and the Bridge Café opposite, now the Curry Kuteer. Firemen used the tower of the Baths for hanging hose-pipes to dry.

THE ROYAL BRINE AND TURKISH BATHS

C1955 / S411004

The Baths, opened by the Duchess of Teck in 1895, used brine recently discovered under Stafford Common during the search for a good water supply. In 1950, prices included 3s for a private brine bath, with a shower 6d extra, 3s 6d for a Turkish bath, and 1s for mixed bathing in the swimming bath.

THE ROYAL BRINE AND TURKISH BATHS

c1955 / S411003

This view is virtually unrecognisable today. The houses on the left remain, but Riverside Recreation Centre now occupies the space behind the trees, and a Tesco supermarket lies to the right. The Civic Restaurant, on the right, opened in 1942 as one of a chain of British Restaurants set up by the Ministry of Food. By the time of this photograph, it was run by the Borough Council and filled 'a great need for the working population, amongst whom it is extremely popular' (Stafford Official Guide) as well as providing school meals.

THE RIVER

c1955 / S411049

Opened in 1914, the library was built with a donation from the Carnegie Trust. It also contained a small museum, and an art gallery was added later. In the centre we can see the Grapes public house, and to the right is the sign for the Sun Inn, behind which was a smithfield, or cattle market.

THE PUBLIC LIBRARY

c1955 / S411018

Two women sit talking on a bench in the gardens, which disappeared in 1962 when a new extension was built. Note the advertising sign for Bamfords farm machinery near the entrance to Woodings agricultural machinery merchants. The adjoining house is now a restaurant. Near here stood the medieval St John's Hospital, an early almshouse, whose patrons were the Stafford family.

THE LIBRARY GARDENS
c1955 / S411025

MARKET SQUARE

C1955 / S411022

A busy scene on the corner of Gaolgate Street, where chain stores such as Woolworth's, Burtons and the Co-operative stand alongside more local shops. A Co-operative Society had been established in Stafford in 1860, and by 1900 it had five branches selling provisions and groceries.

S R Lovatt, on the right, had originally specialised in cheese and in other provisions such as bacon and butter, but as its window display indicates it sold general groceries as well. Liptons, an early example of a chain store, sold similar goods. The clock in front of the garage at the end on Gaol Square replaced a fountain built to commemorate Thomas Sidney, born in the end house on the right. He became a successful merchant, and was Lord Mayor of London in 1853-54. Note the Three Tuns public house with its Joules Stone Ales signs.

STAFFORD

GAOLGATE STREET C1955 / S411021

During the early 1960s, a large area of older buildings behind Gaolgate Street was cleared to build a new modern shopping centre, with a pedestrian way provided with seating. Bookland moved from its Gaolgate Street site and occupied the unit on the left until recently. The Co-operative store on the right sold clothes and groceries.

THE SHOPPING CENTRE

C1965 / S411111

In 1839 Christ Church was opened to cater for the spiritual needs of the expanding suburb of shoe workers to the north of the town. The vicar was also chaplain to the County Lunatic Asylum, the Infirmary and the Workhouse. With declining congregations, it closed in 1976 and was later demolished to make way for a Sheltered Housing scheme.

CHRIST CHURCH

c1965 / S411106

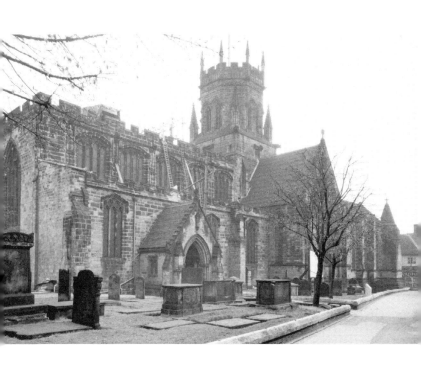

*The building of the church was begun around 1190. The nave of St
Mary's acted as the parish church for the town, while the large chancel
was used by a secular College of Canons, responsible to the King, whose
duty was to pray for members of the royal family. Originally there was a
spire, but it crashed down during a storm in 1594. During the 1840s St
Mary's was heavily restored by George Gilbert Scott, but as the ladders
and scaffolding indicate, there has been a continuing need for roof repairs.
Note the grave slabs and box tombs, and the rear of Brookfields shop
behind the church.*

ST MARY'S CHURCH

c1955 / S411008

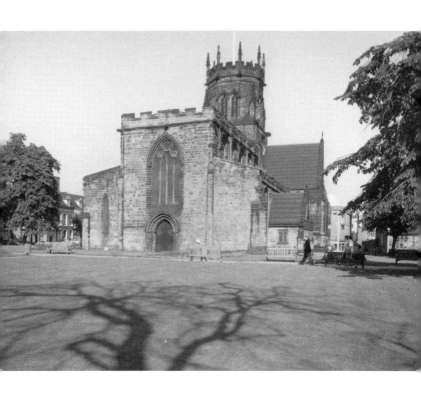

The foundations of the 10th-century church of St Bertelin are laid out adjoining St Mary's behind the middle bench. It stood until 1801, and was used as a grammar school and as the council chamber. The churchyard was levelled and laid out as a garden of remembrance in 1956. A new building, now McDonalds, stands behind the church.

ST MARY'S CHURCH

c1965 / S411114

This borough war memorial was erected in 1922; the soldier points towards the station, from where so many had departed for the Great War. The memorial also bears the names of those killed during the Second World War. The building on the right is the Bird in Hand public house, which seems to have lost its sign.

ST MARY'S CHURCH

c1965 / S411115

These attractive timber-framed buildings are typical of the small dwellings which must have been common in the town in the 16th and 17th centuries. The lane was originally called Bere Lane, and led to the churchyard. St Mary's Church can be seen behind the buildings. An old lamp-post stands at the end of the street.

CHURCH LANE

c1960 / S411099

The Nag's Head public house was one of many around Stafford controlled by Joule's Brewery of Stone, established in the 18th century and closed in 1972. It had a distinctive sign of a red cross on a green background. Note Falaise, a dress shop, and the sign for ice cream at the end of the cobbled pavement.

CHURCH LANE

C1955 / S411098

In the 19th century this area of the town was prone to flooding, and the mill dam was blamed. In 1879 the Corporation bought the mill from Lord Stafford and built a new weir and floodgates. Later, the level of some of the surrounding land was raised, and Victoria Park was opened in 1908.

VICTORIA PARK

c1955 / S411007

This path was laid out in 1880 during the river improvement works. It was named after Izaak Walton, author of 'The Compleat Angler', who was born in Stafford in 1593. In his will he left a farm to his native town, the rent from which was to benefit the poor. Broadeye Windmill can be seen beyond the road bridge.

IZAAK WALTON WALK

C1955 / S411005

47

This bridge across the river, built in 1933, replaced the corroded Victorian structure. The ground here is very soft, and some of the supporting piles extend down eighty feet. The church on the left was St Thomas's, built in 1866 to serve the people of Castletown, who were mainly railway workers. However, the evangelical preaching of its first vicar brought people from other parts of the town, filling the church, and one commentator remarked on the number of 'fine silks and satins with extensive crinolines' to be seen. It closed in 1972, and was demolished.

VICTORIA GARDENS

C1955 / S411015

The park proved so popular that a further extension was created across the river and linked by a new bridge opened in 1911 to commemorate the coronation of George V - hence the name, Coronation Bridge. One of the shelters with its thatched roof can be seen on the left.

VICTORIA GARDENS

c1960 / S411066

The thatched wooden shelter contrasts with the brick refreshment stall,
which does a brisk trade in summer.

VICTORIA PARK

c1960 / S411072

The pleasant gardens of the new park must have provided a welcome contrast to the narrow, cramped streets of small houses which characterised this side of the town. The new extension included a bowling green, which is still in regular use today. The bandstand nearby, which was moved from the Market Square, also still holds concerts in summer.

VICTORIA PARK

c1960 / S411076

This Tenterbanks part of the college was begun in 1937, but the shell of the building was requisitioned by the military and was used as a store by the Americans during the war. A further extension to the park, created in 1930, included the tennis courts seen here on the left, as well as a paddling pool and a children's playground.

THE TECHNICAL COLLEGE

C1955 / S411042

In June 1940, one thousand six hundred evacuee children arrived by train from Ramsgate. First they were taken to Tenterbanks school, seen here on the right, for medical checks; then they went to the Market Hall, where refreshments were provided, before being dispersed to families around Stafford. Some of the older children returned to attend school here, upstairs, while downstairs the local primary schoolgirls continued their lessons. The school was demolished in 1967, and an extension to the college now stands here. The paddling pool in front is still a popular attraction on hot summer days.

VICTORIA GARDENS

c1960 / S411065

THE CHILDREN'S PARK
AND THE OLD MILL

c1955 / S411017

Broadeye Windmill was built in 1796 using material from the Elizabethan Shire Hall, which was then being demolished in the Market Square. It was driven by sails originally, and then a steam engine was installed in 1847 - its chimney stands to the left. By 1880 the windmill was out of use, and was occupied by various shops until 1943. It remained derelict until 1989. It is now being partially restored to open as a small visitor centre. In the foreground is the playground, which opened in 1930. Behind it are small terraced houses, over which towers a large shed of the extensive gas works beyond.

The Stone and Eccleshall roads used to divide in front of the Waggon and Horses public house, but by this time a roundabout had been built to the rear of it, on the left. In front is a row of modern shops, including a Co-operative store at the end by the truck, which had replaced a row of terraced houses. Note the old shoe factory to the right of the Waggon and Horses: at this time it was the Turnpike Hotel and Restaurant. After being partially destroyed by fire, it became a bedding shop - with a flat roof!

STAFFORD
GREYFRIARS c1960 / S411104

PENNYCROFTS COURT

c1965 / S411109

After the Second World War, the Council embarked on a programme of house building. These were the first flats to be built, in 1952, along Corporation Street. They are three-storey, low-rise flats, set well back from the road with room for a bowling green in front.

WINDERMERE HOUSE
c1965 / S411108

These gaunt 19th-century ruins stand on top of the motte built in the late 11th century by Robert of Tosny on land granted to him by William the Conqueror. In 1348 the original timber castle was replaced in stone by Ralph Stafford, a successful soldier and friend of Edward III - he later became Earl of Stafford. In 1334 he had abducted and then married Margaret, an heiress, whose father Hugh Audley died in 1347, providing him with a substantial inheritance.

THE CASTLE

C1955 / S411019

THE CASTLE

c1955 / S411001

The tower of the church dates from the 15th century. There is a carving of the Stafford and the Neville family arms here, suggesting that it may have been built around 1423, when Humphrey, Duke of Buckingham married Anne Neville.

THE CASTLE CHURCH

C1955 / S411045

THE CASTLE

c1955 / S411002

By 1769 the land had passed to the Jerningham family. By 1811 they had started to rebuild the castle in support of their claim to the title of Lord Stafford, but only two towers and some walls were completed. Caretakers remained until the 1950s providing refreshments for visitors, but in 1960, after vandalism and a serious accident, the towers were demolished.

Much of the present church of St Mary, together with the vicarage to the left, dates from the 1840s, when it was virtually rebuilt by George Gilbert Scott. Much of the cost of the rebuilding was borne by George Keen of Rowley Hall, whose daughter had married the vicar, Rev Allen.

THE CASTLE CHURCH

c1955 / S411048

In June 1752, the MP for Stafford, John Robins, married Ann Whitby at Castle Church. A few months later, Sir William Wolseley also claimed to have married her, at Colwich Church! The subsequent publicity and the legal case went on for years, but the vicar of Castle Church was said to have been so upset that he died shortly afterwards.

THE CASTLE CHURCH

C1955 / S411014

How nice if the M6 near Stafford still looked like this today, with so few vehicles, instead of being one of the busiest stretches of motorway in the country! It was opened by the Minister of Transport, Ernest Marples, in 1962, and according to the official opening document, it brought 'long awaited relief to the County Town's congested main street'.

THE M6 MOTORWAY

c1965 / S411101

TIXALL
THE CANAL c1955 / T280002

The impressive Tixall Gatehouse, which we can see beyond the canal, was built by Sir Walter Aston around 1575 in front of his timber-framed hall, long since demolished. Mary, Queen of Scots was held prisoner there for two weeks in 1586 while her rooms at nearby Chartley were searched for evidence of treason against Queen Elizabeth I. She was executed the following year.

Thomas Clifford of Tixall Hall had this half-mile stretch of the Staffordshire and Worcestershire Canal widened to give the impression of a lake in order to improve the view from his house. It provides a good place for sailing, while others prefer to fish from its banks.

TIXALL
THE CANAL C1955 / T280003

Admiral George Anson, born here in 1697, commanded the HMS
'Centurion' on a voyage around the world between 1740 and 1744.
Although many hundreds died, they captured a large Spanish treasure
ship in the Pacific Ocean, from which Anson made his fortune. After his
return he became First Lord of the Admiralty and carried out numerous
naval reforms. On his death in 1762, his brother, Thomas, inherited his
wealth and used some of it to enlarge the family house and landscape
the grounds.

GREAT HAYWOOD

SHUGBOROUGH HALL   c1955 / G303301

This delightful old stone pack-horse bridge has stood here since the 16th century. It is named after the Earls of Essex, who lived at Chartley Hall. Originally it linked Great Haywood to the old village of Shugborough; the village was later removed by the Ansons as it spoiled their view. The angular refuges allowed people to stand aside whilst pack-horses crossed.

GREAT HAYWOOD

ESSEX BRIDGE C1955 / G303018

The Staffordshire and Worcestershire Canal, seen here at its junction with the Trent and Mersey Canal under the bridge, runs to Stourport. Both were built by James Brindley between 1766 and 1777, and they ensured that Staffordshire was at the heart of the canal network. Today the canal basin is a wharf for Anglo-Welsh Narrowboats, and is a busy place again.

GREAT HAYWOOD

THE CANAL c1955 / G303016

This building, from the 1930s, replaced a much earlier inn which had incorporated part of the old gatehouse of Haywood Hall. The name is a reminder of Thomas Clifford, who had married the last of the Aston family of Tixall Hall. The inn had provided accommodation for travellers, and the 'Bed and Breakfast' sign on this building shows that this tradition continued.

GREAT HAYWOOD
THE CLIFFORD ARMS c1955 / G303023

It is hard to believe that this narrow road was once part of one of the major highways of England which had linked London and Chester since medieval times. Its successor, the present A51, now by-passes the village. The Lamb and Flag Hotel, on the left beside the car, was another old inn which catered for travellers.

LITTLE HAYWOOD

THE VILLAGE C1955 / L312014

The Red Lion Inn was rebuilt in the 1930s on the site of a much earlier public house, known from at least the 18th century. Originally called the Bowyer Arms, after the family at Bishton Hall, it was renamed after one of the symbols of their family crest - a rampant red lion, seen on the large sign on the gable.

LITTLE HAYWOOD

THE RED LION c1960 / L312004

Looking down the lane, towards Cannock Chase, note the railway bridge which carried the line between Colwich junction and Macclesfield. It was built in 1848-49 by the North Staffordshire Railway Company (nicknamed the Knotty after its emblem the Stafford Knot), to link local services to the main London line at Colwich. The house on the right has been demolished.

LITTLE HAYWOOD

MEADOW LANE c1955 / L312003

COLWICH

Originally built as a private house called Mount Pleasant in 1730, it was later enlarged and renamed Mount Pavilion. In 1836 it became home to a group of Benedictine nuns. Their community had fled the French Revolution in Paris in 1795 and had settled first in Dorset and then Somerset, before moving to Staffordshire.

According to tradition, the church of St Michael and All Angels is said to stand on the site of a 7th-century wooden chapel dedicated to St Chad. Most of the present church dates from the 19th century, although the tower was built in 1640. There is a memorial inside to Admiral George Anson, who is buried here. Note the St George's flag on the tall flagpole.

COLWICH

THE CHURCH C1955 / C565014A

It was near here in June 1839 that a passenger on a boat to London, Mrs Christina Collins, was brutally beaten, raped and murdered. Her body was dragged out of the canal two days later at the Bloody Steps in Rugeley, where her grave can be seen in the churchyard. Two of the crew were hanged and another transported.

COLWICH

THE LOCK HOUSE c1955 / C565005

The Common has long been a popular place for people to visit at weekends and holidays, and sometimes for fairs and circuses. Some walked or cycled, whilst others took the train, which stopped here until 1950. The Barley Mow public house, on the road to the left, has provided refreshment since at least the early 19th century.

MILFORD

GENERAL VIEW
c1955 / M293022

MILFORD

THE BRIDGE c1955 / M293015

A peaceful scene with cows drinking from the river near the sturdy 18th-century Holdford Bridge, which carries the road from Tixall to Milford. It was near here in the 1880s that the source of a good supply of water was found for Stafford, and a pumping station and hilltop reservoir were built.

During the Great War, Cannock Chase was used as a training area for troops, and two military camps were established at Coppice Hill, near here, and at Brindley Heath, both connected by a railway. In the Second World War an RAF camp was set up at Hednesford. Here, in a more peaceful era, a family are enjoying a quiet picnic.

MILFORD

CANNOCK CHASE c1955 / M293016

This was built by public subscription as a memorial to Sister Dora,
or Dorothy Pattison (1832-78), who was much admired for her work
among the poor in Walsall, especially during a smallpox epidemic there.
The fresh, clear air of Cannock Chase was considered beneficial for
convalescence. Today it is a nursing home for the elderly.

MILFORD

SISTER DORA'S CONVALESCENT HOSPITAL c1955 / M293029

In 1698 the traveller Celia Fiennes noted that there was a considerable industry of cutting and burning the bracken on Cannock Chase. This provided ashes which were made into balls to be used for washing and scouring, many of which were sent to London for use there.

MILFORD

SHERBROOK VALLEY c1955 / M293007

Cannock Chase was originally a royal hunting forest before being sold to the Bishop of Lichfield. By 1560 it was owned by Sir William Paget, who developed an iron smelting industry and deforested much of it for fuel. As we can see here, there has been much replanting during the 20th century, first with conifers and later with mixed woodland.

LITTLE HAYWOOD
SEVEN SPRINGS C1960 / L312012

In 1418-19 John Glasman of Rugeley sent glass to York Minster, and recent excavations nearby have revealed the remains of several glass furnaces dating from the 14th and the 16th centuries. During the 1950s the Chase was declared an Area of Outstanding Natural Beauty, and as these last few photographs have shown, it has been a popular place for recreation.

LITTLE HAYWOOD
THE VIEW FROM THE CHASE c1960 / L312009

RUGELEY

There has been a market in Rugeley since 1259. In 1878 an indoor market hall was built, to the right of this photograph. The two buildings which dominate this view are of very different dates. The bank on the left was built as a private house in 1649, and the Cabin public house was built in 1930-31.

In 1856 a local Rugeley doctor, William Palmer, was convicted of poisoning John Parsons Cook, a race-horse owner, and was hanged outside Stafford Gaol in front of a large crowd. He is thought to have murdered up to fifteen people in this way, including his wife, his mother-in-law, his brother and several of his children. He had insured the lives of some of them, and needed the money to pay off debts he had incurred as a result of his passion for horse-racing. The China Pantry Café and the chemist, with interesting advertising signs, both now demolished, stand on the left.

RUGELEY

BROOK STREET
C1955 / R271029

RUGELEY

BOW STREET c1955 / R271024

The buildings in the foreground still exist, although the offices of the
Rugeley Mercury and the postcard shop have been replaced. Paris House,
with its window display of children's clothes, now sells lighting and gifts,
while Marriot's, a traditional grocer and provision dealers, is now a carpet
shop, having been superseded by large supermarkets.

For several days in June every year this street was thronged with horses and dealers during the annual Horse Fair, when up to one thousand animals were sold. The white building, housing a café and a confectioners, was once a girl's school, while Astbury's was a butcher's shop, which was established in the 19th century. The whole row has now been replaced.

RUGELEY

HORSE FAIR c1955 / R271002x

In the early 19th century, the colliery at Brereton nearby was connected by rail to a wharf, which enabled coal to be transported along the Trent and Mersey canal. Through the trees we can see the roof of the house in which William Palmer was born in 1824. A new bridge now carries traffic on the busy Station Road.

RUGELEY
THE CANAL C1955 / R271047

This has been the home of the Bagot family since 1367, although the building we see here dates from between the 16th and the 19th century. There is a story that Richard II so enjoyed his hunting in the Bagot Park that he presented the family with some black and white goats. Their descendants, known as Bagot goats, remained in the park for many centuries, and some of them can now be seen at Shugborough Park Farm. Much of the land in the valley nearby was flooded in 1953 to create Blithfield Reservoir.

RUGELEY

BLITHFIELD HALL c1955 / R271056

Consecrated in 1848, this was designed by George Gilbert Scott, the architect responsible for the restoration of St Mary's Church in Stafford and many others around the country. Houses now occupy the field where the cows are grazing.

HIXON

ST PETER'S CHURCH c1955 / H412004

In the 19th century the Bank House brewed its own beer: the wall and steps of the malt kiln and the cellar can be seen on the right. Further to the right was a building used for slaughtering animals, but this had ceased by 1904; the building has now been demolished.

HIXON

THE BANK HOUSE HOTEL c1955 / H412011

In 1834 Hixon was described as a 'considerable village of ancient thatched houses'. A public house has stood here since at least the early 19th century. Like many licensees, John Potts, who ran it in 1818, had another occupation as well: he was described as a 'victualler and wheelwright'. Note the unusual key-shaped window and door.

HIXON

THE GREEN MAN INN c1955 / H412009

The name means 'church in a hollow', and there may have been a Christian community here since late Roman times. The Bishops of Lichfield held the estate since at least the 11th century, and possibly much earlier. They made Eccleshall Castle their main residence from around 1200 until 1867. Holy Trinity Church, described by Pevsner as the 'most perfect 13th-century church in the county', reflects this ecclesiastical importance, and six of the Bishops are buried there. The lychgate was erected by parishioners in memory of Colonel Chambers of nearby Walton Hall.

ECCLESHALL

THE CHURCH c1955 / E18001

The bishop was granted the right to hold a weekly market in 1153, and later an annual fair. During the 19th century the market prospered; this new market hall was built for £700, the money having been raised by public subscription. It is now a shop. Note Tompkinson's Garage with its petrol pumps further up the street.

ECCLESHALL

THE VIEW FROM THE CROSS ROADS c1955 / E18006

The main road from London to Chester and Holyhead ran through Eccleshall. When the coaching trade developed around 1800, the town became an important stopping place, and the various inns provided refreshment, accommodation and stabling. One of these, the Crown Hotel, can be seen on the left - its arches provided shelter for the butter market on market days. The wide main street, lined with inns and fine brick buildings, is an indication of its prosperous past in the late 18th and early 19th centuries. The traditional shop front of Moulton's here occupies one of these buildings.

ECCLESHALL
HIGH STREET c1955 / E18005

ECCLESHALL

STAFFORD STREET C1955 / E18011

Gardner's, on the right, was a typical small corner shop, as its window display indicates. At the end on the left beside the vans is the King's Arms, one of the main coaching inns. After the coaching era had ended, it became an excise duty collection point and later the official Inland Revenue premises, as well as remaining as a hotel.

ECCLESHALL

HIGH STREET c1965 / E18033

Like many inn-keepers, the landlord of the Crown Inn was a part-time farmer - he had cowsheds at the back as well as stables. The Crown's kitchens were capable of providing a harvest dinner for over two hundred farmers in 1868, and also the rent dinners for Lord Stafford's estate. It is now a doctor's surgery.

The Royal Oak on the right became one of the two main coaching inns, and had extensive stabling. There is a tradition that Margaret of Anjou, wife of Henry VI, spent the night here before the Battle of Blore Heath in 1459. Ye Olde London House on the left, dated 1717, was the house of a wealthy cloth merchant with London connections. The elaborate petrol pump beside it was for the use of military and other essential vehicles during the war, but it remained there for a long time afterwards.

ECCLESHALL

HIGH STREET C1955 / E18004

Probably built on the site of a Saxon predecessor, the church of St Lawrence displays some of the best 12th-century Norman carving in the county in the crossing arch, which we can just see to the top on each side. Beyond this is the fine 14th-century Decorated east window.

GNOSALL

THE CHURCH, THE NAVE C1955 / G22302

One of the few thatched buildings in the area, the Duke's Head is no longer a public house. It has recently been renovated, and the timber-frame, probably dating from the 16th century, is now exposed. For centuries Gnosall was a small agricultural village, but in the 19th century many of the villagers also made shoes for the Stafford shoe manufacturers.

GNOSALL
HIGH STREET c1955 / G22303

With the opening of the new canal in 1835, a small settlement developed here at Gnosall Heath. The older red brick terrace of houses to the right contrasts with the modern row of shops opposite. Behind these is a council housing estate, Heathways, begun in the early 1950s. Note the unusual road name - Impstones.

GNOSALL
WHARF ROAD c1955 / G22313

The Shropshire Union Canal, engineered by Thomas Telford and constructed between 1827 and 1835, was the last of the major canals. It linked Birmingham to the Mersey, and was built in a more direct line than previous canals, sometimes through deep cuttings, to reduce distances in an attempt to compete with railways. The Boat Inn stands beside the bridge.

GNOSALL
THE CANAL c1960 / G22312

To the south of this bridge is the Cowley Tunnel, the only one on the canal. Although only eighty yards long, it had been intended to make it much longer; but the rock was unstable, and there is a deep cutting beyond instead. New houses now fill the space beyond the Boat Inn, which still provides refreshment for boatmen and local residents.

GNOSALL
WHARF BRIDGE c1955 / G22311

INDEX

PLEASE HELP US BRING FRITH'S PHOTOGRAPHS TO LIFE

Our authors do their best to recount the history of the places they write about. They give insights into how particular towns and villages developed, they describe the architecture of streets and buildings, and they discuss the lives of famous people who lived there. But however knowledgeable our authors are, the story they tell is necessarily incomplete.

Frith's photographs are so much more than plain historical documents. They are living proofs of the flow of human life down the generations. They show real people at real moments in history; and each of those people is the son or daughter of someone, the brother or sister, aunt or uncle, grandfather or grandmother of someone else. All of them lived, worked and played in the streets depicted in Frith's photographs.

We would be grateful if you would tell us about the many places shown in our photographs––the streets with their buildings, shops, businesses and industries. Describe your own memories of life in those streets: what it was like growing up there, who ran the local shop and what shopping was like years ago; if your workplace is shown tell us about your working day and what the building is used for now. With your help more and more Frith photographs can be brought to life, and vital memories preserved for posterity.

We will gradually add your comments and stories to the archive for the benefit of historians of the future. Wherever possible, we will try to include some of your comments in future editions of our books. Moreover, if you spot errors in dates, titles or other facts, please let us know, because our archive records are not always completely accurate—they rely on 150 years of human endeavour and hand-compiled records.

So please write, fax or email us with your stories and memories. Thank you!

FREE PRINT OF YOUR CHOICE

Choose any Frith photograph in this book.
Simply complete the Voucher opposite and
return it with your remittance for £2.25 (to
cover postage and handling) and we will print
the photograph of your choice in SEPIA (size
11 x 8 inches) and supply it in a cream mount
with a burgundy rule line
(overall size 14 x 11 inches).
**Please note: photographs with a reference number
starting with a "Z" are not Frith photographs and
cannot be supplied under this offer.**
Offer valid for delivery to UK one address only.

Mounted Print
Overall size 14 x 11 inches (355 x 280mm)

PLUS: **Order additional Mounted Prints at
HALF PRICE - £7.49 each** (normally £14.99)
If you would like to order more Frith prints
from this book, possibly as gifts for friends and
family, you can buy them at half price (with no
additional postage and handling costs).

PLUS: **Have your Mounted Prints framed**
For an extra £14.95 per print you can have your
mounted print(s) framed in an elegant polished
wood and gilt moulding, overall size
16 x 13 inches (no additional postage and
handling required).

IMPORTANT!

These special prices are only
available if you use this form to
order. You must use the ORIGINAL
VOUCHER (no copies permitted).

We can only despatch to one
UK address. This offer cannot be
combined with any other offer.

FRITH PRODUCTS AND SERVICES

All Frith photographs are available for you to buy as framed or mounted prints.
From time to time, other illustrated items such as Address Books and Maps are also
available. Already, almost 80,000 Frith archive photographs can be viewed and
purchased on the internet through the Frith website.

For more detailed information on Frith companies and products, visit:

www.francisfrith.co.uk

For further information, or trade enquiries, contact:

The Francis Frith Collection, Frith's Barn, Teffont, Salisbury SP3 5QP

Tel: +44 (0) 1722 716 376 Fax: +44 (0) 1722 716 881 Email: sales@francisfrith.co.uk